Native American Life

Igloos

by June Preszler

Consultant:
Troy Rollen Johnson, PhD
American Indian Studies
California State University
Long Beach, California

Mankato, Minnesota

Bridgestone Books are published by Capstone Press,
151 Good Counsel Drive, P.O. Box 669, Mankato, Minnesota 56002.
www.capstonepress.com

Library of Congress Cataloging-in-Publication Data
Preszler, June, 1954–
Igloos / by June Preszler.
    p. cm.—(Bridgestone books. Native American life)
    Includes bibliographical references and index.
    ISBN-13: 978-0-7368-3723-1 (hardcover)
    ISBN-10: 0-7368-3723-X (hardcover)
    1. Igloos. 2. Inuit—Dwellings. I. Title. II. Series: Bridgestone Books: Native American life
(Mankato, Minn.)
E99.E7P74 2005
728'.089'971—dc22
                                        2004011213

Summary: A brief introduction to igloos, including the materials, construction, and people who lived in
these traditional Native American dwellings.

Editorial Credits
Roberta Basel and Katy Kudela, editors; Jennifer Bergstrom, designer; Wanda Winch, photo researcher;
Scott Thoms, photo editor

Photo Credits
Aurora/Joanna B. Pinneo, 20
Corbis/Bettmann, 6
Getty Images Inc./Wayne R. Bilenduke, 14
Nature Picture Library/Doug Allan, 4; Martha Holmes, 10
Photo Researchers Inc./Bryan & Cherry Alexander Photography, cover, 1, 8, 16, 18
SuperStock, 12

1 2 3 4 5 6 10 09 08 07 06 05

Table of Contents

What Is an Igloo?

Igloos are houses built in the shape of a dome. They can be made from sod, wood, or snow. Some Native Americans in the northern part of North America built snow igloos.

People built snow igloos of different sizes. Some igloos had room for only one person. Others were large enough for a family.

Many snow igloos had a window and a porch. The porch looked like a tunnel. It helped keep out cold air. People crawled through the porch to get inside the igloo.

◀ Snow igloos are one kind of igloo. They are shaped like a dome.

Who Lived in an Igloo?

The Inuit lived in igloos. The Inuit are a Native American group. Years ago, the Inuit were called Eskimo. The Inuit lived in the Arctic from central Alaska to northern Canada.

The Inuit used igloos on hunting trips. People in the coldest areas of the Arctic lived in igloos all winter.

Today, many Inuit still live in the northern areas of North America. Few Inuit live in snow igloos. They sometimes build snow igloos for hunting trips.

◀ Snow igloos gave the Inuit shelter from the wind and snow.

Gathering Materials

The Inuit became known for their snow igloos. They made the igloos with blocks of snow.

Builders made their igloos out of hard, wind-packed snow. They used a knife to cut the snow into blocks. The knife was made of bone, metal, or **ivory**.

There are many kinds of snow. The Inuit tried to use snow from the same snowfall. Using different kinds of snow could lead to cracks in the igloo.

◄ The Inuit used knives to cut blocks of snow from the ground. Today some builders use saws.

Preparing the Site

An Inuit hunter often built a small igloo by himself. He first chose a flat spot. Next, he drew a circle in the snow to show the size of the igloo. He marked a circle just big enough to allow himself to lie down in it.

People worked together to build larger snow igloos. Family igloos were 6 to 15 feet (2 to 5 meters) wide.

◄ An Inuit hunter could build a small snow igloo alone.

Building an Igloo

The builder first laid blocks of snow end to end. The blocks followed the circle drawn in the snow. The builder then stacked blocks in a dome shape. The last block placed was the **keystone**. This block held all the other pieces in place. The builder cut a small hole in the top of the dome for a chimney.

Melting the surface snow was the last step. The builder used an oil lamp to melt a thin layer of snow on the inside of the igloo. The melted snow froze into ice. This ice layer helped keep out the wind.

◀ A builder carefully placed each snow block to form a dome shape.

Inside an Igloo

Inside their family igloos, the Inuit spent time together. They cooked meals and sewed. They also told stories and sang.

Family igloos often had two or three **platforms**. One platform was covered with willow mats topped by furs or moss. The Inuit slept on these mats.

An oil lamp sat on a platform by the door. The Inuit used the lamp for heat and for cooking.

◄ Inuit families spent time together in their igloo homes. They often shared stories and sang songs.

Igloo Villages

In some parts of Canada, the Inuit built igloo villages. They lived in the igloos during the winter months. As many as 300 people lived in one village.

Families and friends sometimes built tunnels joining igloos together. People could crawl through the tunnels to visit each other. They did not need to walk outside.

◄ Some Inuit built snow igloos close together to form a village.

Special Igloos

Special igloos were sometimes built for **ceremonies** and dances. In Thule, Greenland, the Inuit built large igloos called snow domes. People in the village often gathered there during long winter nights. They held singing, dancing, and wrestling events in these igloos.

◄ The Inuit built large igloos for special events.

Keeping Warm

The Inuit stayed very warm inside their snow igloos. During the day, the sun shone through the layer of ice and lit the home. A **blubber** oil lamp could warm the igloo to 90 degrees Fahrenheit (32 degrees Celsius). Some Inuit also covered the inside walls with animal furs. The furs helped keep the house warm.

In winter, some people still build snow igloos for warmth. During long trips across Canada, people use snow igloos for shelter.

◄ Heat from an oil lamp helped the Inuit keep warm inside their snow igloos.

Glossary

blubber (BLUH-bur)—fat under the skin of a whale or a seal; the Inuit used oil made from blubber to light their lamps.

ceremony (SER-uh-moh-nee)—formal actions, words, and often music performed to mark an important occasion

ivory (EYE-vur-ee)—the natural substance from which the tusks and teeth of some animals are made

keystone (KEE-stone)—the wedge-shaped piece at the top of the igloo that locks the other blocks of snow in place

platform (PLAT-form)—a flat, raised structure where people can stand or sleep

Read More

Cordoba, Yasmine A. *Igloo.* Native American Homes. Vero Beach, Fla.: Rourke, 2001.

Williams, Suzanne M. *The Inuit.* Watts Library. New York: Franklin Watts, 2003.

Internet Sites

FactHound offers a safe, fun way to find Internet sites related to this book. All of the sites on FactHound have been researched by our staff.

Here's how:
1. Visit *www.facthound.com*
2. Type in this special code **073683723X** for age-appropriate sites. Or enter a search word related to this book for a more general search.
3. Click on the **Fetch It** button.

FactHound will fetch the best sites for you!

Index